Repertory

of Jungian

Archetypes & Complexes

Written & Compiled

By

Peter Twigg

Acknowledgements

Sed ad gloriam nominis tui, C.G. Jung.

To the many others who have built on Carl Jung's work including Marie-Louise von Franz, Edward Edinger, Jeffrey Raff, James Hollis, Robert Johnson, and so many others who have helped shape the field of Analytical Psychology.

And to three people who have shaped my life, Dr. Philip Groves, Kane Parsons and Brett Traynor.

First published in 2026 by print on demand. This book best serves as a Repertory and stand-alone Ready Reckoner for easy access. There are no digital editions of this book.

ISBN: 978-0-6459989-2-4

Contents

About this Book

This Repertory is a systematic reference organised so that you can enter from any angle and find what you need quickly. Its subject is the Archetypes and Complexes of Jungian psychology, presented in a consistent format designed for recognition, study, and recall.

The Repertory is organised in two halves. The first covers Archetypes, grouped into three clusters: the Structural Core (the foundational psychic structures — Self, Ego, Persona, Shadow, Anima, and Animus), the Dynamic Core (the developmental and archetypal figures — Puer, Puella, Senex, Child, Divine Child, and Wounded Child), and the Extended Archetypes (Hero, Trickster, Father, Great Father, Terrible Father, Mother, Great Mother, Terrible Mother, Kore/Maiden, Persephone, and the Wise Old Man/Woman). The second half covers Complexes, organised by type: Family, Gender-Related, Power and Identity, Relationship, and Psychological Defence. A reference table at the close maps the key Archetype-to-Complex relationships.

Every entry follows the same five-part structure: Core Essence, Positive/Mature Potentials, Negative/Immature Expressions, Typical Behaviours & Patterns, and Developmental Task, followed by Notes. This consistency is intentional — once you are familiar with the format, you can move through any entry efficiently and know exactly where to look for what you need.

The Repertory is designed for beginner and intermediate students. Use it as a ready reckoner when you encounter an unfamiliar term, as a study text when you want to absorb a particular Archetype or Complex in depth, or as a quick clinical reference when you need to identify a constellation from its observable features. You are invited to play with it — to browse, cross-reference, and return to entries as your understanding deepens.

A word on scope: the Repertory gives you the shape of each Archetype and Complex — it's essential features, its potentials, its pitfalls, and the developmental work it calls for. It is not a substitute for reading the primary literature. The depth required to work proficiently with these forces in a clinical or personal context comes from engaging directly with the collected works of C. G. Jung, Marie-Louise von Franz, and other recognised Jungian scholars. The Repertory opens the door; the primary texts build the house. This Repertory draws exclusively from the classical Jungian canon — principally the Collected Works of C. G. Jung, and the interpretive scholarship of Marie-Louise von Franz, Erich Neumann, and Edward Edinger. Post-Jungian developments — including the archetypal frameworks of James Hillman, Robert Moore, Douglas Gillette, and others — have extended and enriched the field considerably. These are not absent from the tradition, but they lie beyond the scope of this Repertory, which aims to offer the reader a secure grounding in the original Jungian framework before engaging with its subsequent elaborations.

To assist the student and beginning practitioner in moving from this Repertory into the primary literature, each entry carries superscript reference markers alongside its five structural elements: Core Essence, Positive / Mature Potentials, Negative / Immature Expressions, Typical Behaviours & Patterns, and Developmental Task. These markers cite Jung's Collected Works by paragraph number (§) — consistent across all editions and publishers, and the precise point at which your own reading of Jung begins. The interpretive scholarship of von Franz, Neumann, and Edinger is named at the foot of each entry, in the Reference line, at the level of the work itself: you are pointed to the book to take up and read, not to a page to extract from. The citation conventions are set out in the Citation Style Guide at the back of this volume.

The Archetypes in this Repertory are organised into three groupings. The Core Archetypes — the Self, Ego, Persona, Shadow, Anima, and Animus — are the structural foundations of the psyche: the universal patterns that organise inner life at the deepest level. The Dynamic Archetypes — the Puer, Puella, Senex, Child, Divine Child, and Wounded Child — are the developmental and energic forces that move the psyche through time. The Extended Archetypes — the Hero, Trickster, Father, Great Father, Terrible Father, Mother, Great Mother, Terrible Mother, Kore/Maiden, Persephone, and the Wise Old Man/Woman — are the culturally elaborated expressions of archetypal energy: the recurring characters through which the deeper patterns clothe themselves in image and story.

Within several entries, the Repertory identifies a quality particular to Jungian psychology: that some archetypal figures carry two faces — two expressions of the same underlying energy that appear to be opposites but are, at depth, aspects of one whole. This applies to the Child, the Mother, the Father, and the Kore. Understanding these as two faces of one figure — not separate archetypes — is central to the Jungian view: what appears as opposition at the surface is, at depth, always an expression of wholeness seeking integration. A note on each pairing follows the relevant entries in this Repertory.

Core Archetypes

The Structural Core

The Self

CORE ESSENCE

The totality and organising centre of the psyche; the principle of wholeness that transcends the ego.[CW 9ii §§43–44]

POSITIVE / MATURE POTENTIALS

- Psychological wholeness
- Integration of conscious and unconscious
- Inner unity and coherence
- Alignment with deeper meaning and purpose
- Stable inner centre
- Capacity to hold opposites
- Authentic self-expression
- Spiritual grounding in reality
- Inner authority not dependent on validation
- Deep intuitive guidance
- Acceptance of paradox
- Integration of shadow aspects
- Emotional balance and depth
- Sense of meaning beyond ego
- Capacity for inner stillness[CW 9ii §§44–45, §59–60]

NEGATIVE / IMMATURE EXPRESSIONS

- Inflation — identifying as "whole" or "realised"
- Spiritual grandiosity
- Identification with an idealised self-image
- Detachment from ordinary human reality

- Spiritual bypassing
- Avoidance of unresolved psychological material
- False sense of completion
- Dissociation masked as transcendence
- Loss of ego boundaries
- Subtle superiority over others
- Confusion between ego and Self
- Collapse into passivity
- Avoidance of conflict under the guise of unity[CW 9ii §45; CW 9i §§44–46]

TYPICAL BEHAVIOURS / PATTERNS

- Speaks in universal truths without grounding in personal reality
- Avoids personal psychological work
- Claims insight without embodiment
- Positions self as "beyond" ordinary concerns
- Drawn to peak or unity experiences
- Alternates between genuine clarity and grandiose inflation[CW 9ii §45]

DEVELOPMENTAL TASK

Differentiate ego from Self; integrate shadow and unconscious material, ground insight in lived reality, and hold the tension of wholeness and human limitation simultaneously — with humility.[CW 9ii §§45, 67]

Reference: Jung, C.G. — Aion, CW 9ii; Edinger, E.F. — Ego and Archetype.

NOTES

The Ego

CORE ESSENCE

The centre of conscious identity; responsible for orientation, decision-making, and functioning in reality.[CW 9ii §§1–2]

POSITIVE / MATURE POTENTIALS

- Stable sense of identity
- Reality orientation
- Decision-making capacity
- Personal responsibility
- Boundary formation
- Coherent self-concept
- Ability to plan and act
- Adaptability to circumstances
- Reflective awareness
- Accountability
- Resilience under pressure
- Functional independence
- Clear communication
- Goal-directed behaviour
- Capacity for self-regulation[CW 9ii §§5, 11]

NEGATIVE / IMMATURE EXPRESSIONS

- Over-identification with identity or roles
- Rigidity and inflexibility
- Defensiveness
- Fear of loss of control
- Ego inflation — self-importance
- Ego fragility — collapse under pressure
- Denial of unconscious material
- Control-based behaviour
- Need for validation

- Resistance to change
- Narrow perception of reality
- Chronic comparison with others
- Over-reliance on rational control[CW 9ii §§7–9]

TYPICAL BEHAVIOURS / PATTERNS

- Defends identity when challenged
- Seeks control over situations and people
- Avoids uncertainty
- Reacts strongly to criticism
- Clings to established self-image
- Over-plans or over-corrects to maintain a sense of order[CW 9ii §§7–8]

DEVELOPMENTAL TASK

Learn to relate to — rather than dominate — the psyche; accept the limits of control, open genuinely to unconscious material, and develop the flexibility and humility to strengthen without inflating.[CW 9ii §§9–12]

Reference: Jung, C.G. — Aion, CW 9ii; Edinger, E.F. — Ego and Archetype.

NOTES

The Persona

CORE ESSENCE

The social mask or role adopted in response to outer demands; the functional interface between the individual and the external world.[CW 7 §§243–245]

POSITIVE / MATURE POTENTIALS

- Appropriate social adaptation
- Professional and social competence
- Ability to meet contextual role demands
- Flexibility in self-presentation across contexts
- Social intelligence
- Capacity to navigate diverse social environments
- Protective function for the inner life
- Healthy containment of the private from the public
- Cultural and professional effectiveness
- Self-respect within social roles
- Capacity to modulate expression appropriately[CW 7 §§246–249]

NEGATIVE / IMMATURE EXPRESSIONS

- Over-identification with the role or mask
- Loss of authentic self beneath the performance
- Inability to remove the mask in intimate contexts
- Social conformity at the expense of individuality
- Persona collapse under pressure or direct challenge
- Chronic performance anxiety
- Rigidity in role behaviour
- Dependence on external recognition for self-worth
- Inner emptiness beneath the social face
- Inability to be known as oneself
- Shallow relating — connection only at the surface level[CW 7 §§249–252]

TYPICAL BEHAVIOURS / PATTERNS

- Presents markedly differently across different contexts
- Struggles to "be themselves" outside of defined roles
- Reacts intensely when role or status is not recognised
- Uses appearance, title, or position to define personal worth
- Feels disoriented or empty when stripped of professional identity
- Avoids intimacy that would require dropping the mask[CW 7 §§249–252]

DEVELOPMENTAL TASK

Distinguish between the social role and the authentic self; wear the mask with conscious choice as a functional interface, recognising it as a means of engagement — not a substitute for identity.[CW 7 §§252–253]

Reference: Jung, C.G. — Two Essays on Analytical Psychology, CW 7.

NOTES

The Shadow

CORE ESSENCE

The rejected, repressed, or unconscious aspects of the personality; everything the ego has denied, refused to own, or expelled from awareness.[CW 9ii §§13–14]

POSITIVE / MATURE POTENTIALS

- Access to vitality and instinctual energy
- Psychological depth
- Authentic emotional expression
- Creativity drawn from unconscious material
- Honesty about one's darker aspects
- Increased self-awareness
- Integration of instinctual life
- Strength through self-confrontation
- Capacity for transformation
- Grounded realism about human nature
- Boundary clarity
- Reduction of projection
- Emotional resilience
- Expanded sense of self[CW 9ii §§16–17]

NEGATIVE / IMMATURE EXPRESSIONS

- Projection onto others
- Denial of personal responsibility
- Repressed anger or desire
- Emotional outbursts
- Self-sabotage
- Destructive impulses
- Passive-aggressive behaviour
- Victim mentality
- Moral hypocrisy

- Unconscious manipulation
- Addictive tendencies
- Fear-driven reactions
- Splitting — all-good or all-bad thinking[CW 9ii §§15–16]

TYPICAL BEHAVIOURS / PATTERNS

- Strong reactions to traits in others that are disowned in the self
- Repeating destructive patterns without awareness
- Hidden motives driving behaviour
- Acting "out of character" under stress
- Blaming others for internal emotional states
- Strong attraction to those who embody disowned traits[CW 9ii §§17–18]

DEVELOPMENTAL TASK

Acknowledge and own all disowned aspects; withdraw projections, integrate instinct and emotion, take full responsibility for the inner life, and transform destructive energy into conscious, purposeful action.[CW 9ii §§17–19]

Reference: Jung, C.G. — Aion, CW 9ii; von Franz, M.-L. — Shadow and Evil in Fairy Tales; Edinger, E.F. — Ego and Archetype.

NOTES

The Anima (in men)

CORE ESSENCE

The inner feminine image in a man; mediates emotion, relatedness, and connection to the unconscious.[CW 9i §§55–66; CW 7 §§296–300]

POSITIVE / MATURE POTENTIALS

- Emotional awareness
- Capacity for intimacy
- Empathy and compassion
- Sensitivity to inner states
- Imagination and creativity
- Intuitive perception
- Relational depth
- Receptivity to the unconscious
- Aesthetic appreciation
- Capacity for love and connection
- Psychological openness
- Inner reflection
- Symbolic thinking
- Spiritual receptivity[CW 9ii §§33, 40; CW 7 §374; CW 12 §242]

NEGATIVE / IMMATURE EXPRESSIONS

- Moodiness and emotional instability
- Emotional dependency
- Idealisation of women
- Projection of the inner image onto partners
- Irrational emotional reactions
- Seductive manipulation
- Passivity
- Escapism into fantasy
- Over-sensitivity
- Loss of direction

- Emotional engulfment
- Romantic delusion[CW 9i §§59, 115, 144, 357; CW 7 §§310–320]

TYPICAL BEHAVIOURS / PATTERNS

- Falls in love with projections rather than real persons
- Seeks completion and wholeness through relationships
- Over-identifies with emotional states
- Alternates between idealisation and disappointment
- Uses emotion to avoid action or responsibility[CW 9i §§57, 356–357]

DEVELOPMENTAL TASK

Withdraw projections from women, develop a genuine inner relationship with the feeling function, integrate emotion with purposeful action, and relate consciously to the feminine principle within.[CW 9i §§146–147; CW 7 §§323f, 374, 384; CW 9ii §§33, 40]

Reference: Jung, C.G. — The Archetypes and the Collective Unconscious, CW 9i; von Franz, M.-L. — The Feminine in Fairy Tales; Edinger, E.F. — Ego and Archetype.

NOTES

The Animus (in women)

CORE ESSENCE

The inner masculine image in a woman; mediates thought, direction, and assertion.[CW 9i §63; CW 9ii §§28–30; CW 7 §§328–332]

POSITIVE / MATURE POTENTIALS

- Clarity of thought
- Discernment
- Inner authority
- Decisiveness
- Assertiveness
- Capacity for structure and direction
- Logical reasoning
- Independence
- Goal orientation
- Leadership capacity
- Boundary setting
- Objective thinking
- Persistence[CW 9ii §§33–35; CW 7 §§336–337]

NEGATIVE / IMMATURE EXPRESSIONS

- Rigidity of thought
- Opinionated certainty
- Over-criticism
- Argumentative behaviour
- Domineering tendencies
- Disconnection from feeling
- Harsh inner dialogue
- Projection onto men
- Control-based relating
- Intellectual arrogance
- Rejection of vulnerability

- Polarised thinking[CW 9ii §§28–30; CW 7 §§333–336]

TYPICAL BEHAVIOURS / PATTERNS

- Argues from fixed, unmovable positions
- Over-relies on being "right"
- Dismisses emotional nuance as weakness
- Projects authority and power onto external men
- Uses intellect to dominate or defend against intimacy[CW 9ii §29; CW 7 §335]

DEVELOPMENTAL TASK

Differentiate the inner voice from projection onto men; integrate thinking with feeling, develop genuine flexibility of mind, and balance assertion with receptivity — relating to inner authority consciously.[CW 9ii §§33, 40; CW 7 §§337–340]

Reference: Jung, C.G. — The Archetypes and the Collective Unconscious, CW 9i; von Franz, M.-L. — The Feminine in Fairy Tales; Edinger, E.F. — Ego and Archetype.

NOTES

The Dynamic Core

Puer Aeternus (Eternal Youth)

CORE ESSENCE

The archetype of eternal youth; represents possibility, spirit, and the resistance to limitation and grounding.[CW 9i §§278, 281]

POSITIVE / MATURE POTENTIALS

- Visionary orientation
- Openness to possibility
- Creativity and imagination
- Adaptability
- Playfulness and vitality
- Courage to break convention
- Intuitive insight
- Capacity for reinvention
- Enthusiasm and inspiration
- Non-attachment to rigid identity
- Exploration and risk-taking
- Sensitivity to meaning
- Lightness of being[CW 9i §289]

NEGATIVE / IMMATURE EXPRESSIONS

- Avoidance of responsibility
- Fear of limitation and commitment
- Chronic instability in life direction
- Escapism into fantasy or spirituality
- Lack of follow-through
- Dependency masked as freedom
- Rejection of structure
- Impulsivity

- Addiction to novelty
- Spiritual bypassing
- Living in potential rather than reality[CW 9i §285]

TYPICAL BEHAVIOURS / PATTERNS

- Starts projects but rarely completes them
- Avoids long-term commitments
- Seeks peak experiences as a substitute for sustained engagement
- Idealises new paths and then abandons them
- Resists routine and structure as threats to freedom[CW 9i §285]

DEVELOPMENTAL TASK

Accept limitation and the necessity of structure; build discipline and continuity, enter grounded life fully, and integrate with the Senex to transform boundless possibility into lived, embodied reality.[CW 9i §293]

Reference: Jung, C.G. — The Archetypes and the Collective Unconscious, CW 9i (The Psychology of the Child Archetype); von Franz, M.-L. — Puer Aeternus; Edinger, E.F. — Ego and Archetype.

NOTES

Puella Aeterna (Eternal Maiden)

CORE ESSENCE

The feminine expression of eternal youth; embodies emotional openness, feeling, and boundless possibility without grounding or commitment.[CW 9i §§278, 311]

POSITIVE / MATURE POTENTIALS

- Emotional openness
- Sensitivity and receptivity
- Imagination and creativity
- Openness to change
- Playfulness
- Capacity for wonder
- Romantic appreciation of life
- Intuitive perception
- Psychological flexibility
- Ability to inspire hope in others
- Spiritual receptivity
- Capacity for renewal and reinvention[CW 9i §316]

NEGATIVE / IMMATURE EXPRESSIONS

- Avoidance of responsibility and commitment
- Fear of limitation, structure, and grounded reality
- Chronic indecision and inability to follow through
- Escapism into fantasy, spirituality, or idealism
- Dependency on others for stability or direction
- Emotional volatility and hypersensitivity
- Naivety and lack of discernment
- Addiction to novelty, change, or intensity
- Romantic delusion — seeing life as it "should be"
- Lack of boundaries or psychological containment
- Passive waiting for life rather than active participation

- Fear of aging, maturity, and embodiment
- Remaining the potential rather than becoming actual[CW 9i §355]

TYPICAL BEHAVIOURS / PATTERNS

- Waits rather than acts; seeks emotional rescue
- Avoids grounded, sustained responsibility
- Idealises relationships and life circumstances
- Fluctuates emotionally without resolution
- Resists maturity as a threat to aliveness[CW 9i §§311, 355]

DEVELOPMENTAL TASK

Develop genuine grounding and autonomy; build firm boundaries, take full responsibility for one's own life, integrate feeling with action, and move from endless potential into actual, embodied reality.[CW 9i §§316, 355]

Reference: Jung, C.G. — The Archetypes and the Collective Unconscious, CW 9i (The Psychological Aspects of the Kore); von Franz, M.-L. — The Feminine in Fairy Tales; Edinger, E.F. — Ego and Archetype.

NOTES

Senex (The Old Man)

CORE ESSENCE

The archetype of structure, order, limitation, and earned wisdom; the balancing counterpart to the Puer and Puella.[CW 9i §§384–396]

POSITIVE / MATURE POTENTIALS

Constructive expression of the senex principle is treated under Wise Old Man, where Jung develops the positive pole directly.

Jung and von Franz did not develop a positive pole for the Senex. For its constructive expression — wisdom, discernment, the containing elder — see the Wise Old Man / Wise Old Woman. (The positive Senex as an explicit polarity is post-Jungian — see Hillman — beyond this volume's scope.)

NEGATIVE / IMMATURE EXPRESSIONS

- Rigidity
- Cynicism
- Over-control
- Emotional suppression
- Fear of change
- Authoritarian tendencies
- Harsh judgment
- Stagnation
- Lifeless routine
- Resistance to new ideas
- Coldness
- Excessive seriousness

TYPICAL BEHAVIOURS / PATTERNS

- Prioritises structure over vitality and aliveness
- Resists change and innovation
- Dismisses new or unconventional ideas
- Over-values discipline at the expense of spontaneity

- Judges or dismisses playfulness and lightness

DEVELOPMENTAL TASK

Integrate vitality, openness, and the spirit of renewal; soften rigidity and allow new possibility, balancing the earned wisdom of structure with the living energy of the Puer and Puella.

Reference: Jung, C.G. — The Archetypes and the Collective Unconscious, CW 9i (The Phenomenology of the Spirit in Fairy Tales); von Franz, M.-L. — Puer Aeternus; Edinger, E.F. — Ego and Archetype.

NOTES

The Child

CORE ESSENCE

The original state of the psyche; represents potential, vulnerability, and the unformed nature of early psychological development.[CW 9i §§259–260]

POSITIVE / MATURE POTENTIALS

- Openness
- Curiosity
- Emotional authenticity
- Spontaneity
- Trust
- Imagination
- Capacity for joy
- Sensitivity
- Learning capacity
- Psychological flexibility
- Presence[CW 9i §§278, 289]

NEGATIVE / IMMATURE EXPRESSIONS

- Dependency
- Fearfulness
- Emotional overwhelm
- Lack of boundaries
- Regression
- Naivety
- Impulsivity
- Avoidance of responsibility
- Fragility
- Clinging behaviour
- Victim orientation[CW 9i §§270, 285]

TYPICAL BEHAVIOURS / PATTERNS

- Seeks safety and external approval
- Reacts emotionally before thinking
- Avoids difficulty and discomfort
- Looks to others for direction and permission
- Alternates between play and emotional distress[CW 9i §§285, 289]

DEVELOPMENTAL TASK

Develop genuine autonomy and ego strength, build appropriate boundaries, and integrate the tension between dependence and independence — growing into adulthood without losing the original vitality, curiosity, and openness.[CW 9i §§293, 305]

Reference: Jung, C.G. — The Archetypes and the Collective Unconscious, CW 9i; von Franz, M.-L. — The Interpretation of Fairy Tales; Edinger, E.F. — Ego and Archetype.

NOTES

Note on Two Faces: The Child

The Child archetype carries two faces in Jungian psychology, both of which appear as separate entries in this Repertory.[CW 9i §§259–305]

The Divine Child is the forward-facing face — the symbol of future wholeness and emergent possibility, the nascent Self not yet realised. It carries the sense of destiny, renewal, and creative potential. It is what the psyche is moving toward.

The Wounded Child is the backward-facing face — the aspect of the psyche shaped by early psychological injury, carrying the memory of wounding and the patterns formed in response to it. It is what the psyche is still carrying.

These are not opposites — they are the same figure seen from different positions in time. The wound marks the place where unrealised potential was forced underground; the Divine Child is that potential seeking expression. Healing does not erase the wound — it transforms it into the doorway through which the emerging Self passes. Both must be encountered honestly: the Wounded Child cannot be bypassed in favour of the Divine Child's promise, nor can the Divine Child's vision be dismissed as mere fantasy. Integration requires holding both faces of the same Child.

Reference: Jung, C.G. — The Archetypes and the Collective Unconscious, CW 9i (The Psychology of the Child Archetype); von Franz, M.-L. — The Interpretation of Fairy Tales; Edinger, E.F. — Ego and Archetype.

The Divine Child

CORE ESSENCE

The symbol of future wholeness and emergent possibility; the nascent Self not yet realised, carrying the potential of transformation.[CW 9i §§267, 281]

POSITIVE / MATURE POTENTIALS

- Carrier of transformation potential
- Symbol of renewal and new life
- Inner guiding image of the emerging Self
- Creative emergence
- Connection to deeper Self
- Future-oriented developmental energy[CW 9i §§278, 289, 293]

NEGATIVE / IMMATURE EXPRESSIONS

- Inflation — identifying as "special" or chosen
- Fragility when ordinary development is required
- Avoidance of actual development in favour of imagined destiny
- Identification with potential only, never actuality
- Spiritual idealisation as a defence against effort[CW 9i §§285, 289]

TYPICAL BEHAVIOURS / PATTERNS

- Feels destined for something significant but remains inactive
- Identifies as unique or chosen without earned basis
- Avoids the ordinary work of development
- Seeks profound meaning without grounding in reality[CW 9i §§278, 289]

DEVELOPMENTAL TASK

Ground the sense of future potential in present, sustained effort; develop through ordinary commitment and discipline, integrate genuine humility, and move from imagining greatness to actually becoming it.[CW 9i §§291, 293]

Reference: Jung, C.G. — The Archetypes and the Collective Unconscious, CW 9i (The Psychology of the Child Archetype); von Franz, M.-L. — The Interpretation of Fairy Tales; Edinger, E.F. — Ego and Archetype.

NOTES

The Wounded Child

CORE ESSENCE

The aspect of the psyche shaped by early psychological injury; carries the memory of wounding and organises behaviour around unresolved pain.[CW 9i §§270, 285]

POSITIVE / MATURE POTENTIALS

- Emotional depth
- Empathy born of experience
- Sensitivity
- Psychological insight
- Motivation for genuine growth
- Authenticity[CW 9i §285]

NEGATIVE / IMMATURE EXPRESSIONS

- Victim identity as a fixed orientation
- Chronic emotional reactivity
- Dependency
- Compulsive repetition of wound patterns
- Fear of abandonment
- Self-sabotage
- Regression under stress[CW 9i §§270, 285]

TYPICAL BEHAVIOURS / PATTERNS

- Reacts strongly and disproportionately to perceived rejection
- Seeks external validation to manage inner instability
- Repeats destructive relational patterns
- Lives from past emotional memory rather than present reality
- Alternates between desperate neediness and defensive withdrawal[CW 9i §§270, 285]

DEVELOPMENTAL TASK

Process early psychological wounds with honesty and care; build emotional regulation and adult responsibility, stop projecting the past onto the present, and integrate the pain as a source of depth, empathy, and genuine strength.[CW 9i §§285, 293]

Reference: Jung, C.G. — The Archetypes and the Collective Unconscious, CW 9i (The Psychology of the Child Archetype); Edinger, E.F. — Ego and Archetype.

NOTES

Extended Archetypes

The Hero

CORE ESSENCE

The archetype of the ego's journey through challenge and transformation; the psychic force that meets the unknown, endures the ordeal, and returns with earned capacity.[CW 5 §§251, 612]

POSITIVE / MATURE POTENTIALS

- Courage in the face of the unknown
- Willingness to enter difficulty and suffering
- Determination and persistence under pressure
- Strength of character forged through ordeal
- Capacity to protect and serve
- Initiative and decisive action
- Resilience through failure
- Growth achieved through genuine trial
- Moral fortitude
- Achievement of genuine individuation
- Inspiration and leadership to others
- Capacity to face the Shadow directly[CW 5 §§259, 398, 415]

NEGATIVE / IMMATURE EXPRESSIONS

- Over-identification with the heroic role — inability to rest or receive
- Chronic need for challenge or conflict to feel alive
- Inability to acknowledge vulnerability
- Suppression of the inner feminine (Anima)
- Arrogance born of past achievement
- Compulsive rescuing of others
- Isolation — the lone hero who cannot bond
- Grandiosity and inflation after victory

- Treating ordinary life as beneath them
- Fear of the return — difficulty integrating the journey
- Driven by wound rather than genuine calling[CW 5 §§392, 460]

TYPICAL BEHAVIOURS / PATTERNS

- Throws self into challenge before reflecting
- Finds meaning primarily through struggle or mission
- Struggles to receive help — must face the dragon alone
- Drives forward when rest or integration is needed
- Defines self through what has been overcome[CW 5 §§375, 553]

DEVELOPMENTAL TASK

Recognise that the greatest heroic act is ultimately the surrender of heroism itself; integrate vulnerability, receive help, return from the journey, and find courage in the ordinary as much as in the extraordinary.[CW 5 §§415, 524, 612]

Reference: Jung, C.G. — Symbols of Transformation, CW 5; von Franz, M.-L. — The Interpretation of Fairy Tales; Edinger, E.F. — Ego and Archetype.

NOTES

The Trickster

CORE ESSENCE

The archetype of disruption, paradox, and the subversion of fixed order; mediates between conscious and unconscious through cunning, humour, and the creative power of chaos.[CW 9i §§456, 472]

POSITIVE / MATURE POTENTIALS

- Creative disruption of rigid patterns
- Capacity to reveal what is hidden through humour
- Flexibility and psychological agility
- Ability to expose hypocrisy and pretension
- Disrupting rigid boundaries to release creative vitality
- Capacity to hold paradox and ambiguity
- Liberation from convention and fixed thinking
- Insight arrived at through unexpected angles
- Cultural and psychological renewal
- Access to the liminal and the threshold
- Ability to make the unsayable sayable[CW 9i §§465, 472]

NEGATIVE / IMMATURE EXPRESSIONS

- Manipulation without conscience
- Deception and betrayal
- Chaos pursued for its own sake
- Exploitation of others' vulnerabilities
- Avoidance of accountability through humour
- Inability to be serious when gravity is required
- Compulsive subversion of all authority regardless of merit
- Mischief that wounds rather than illuminates
- Living outside ethical boundaries
- Projection of earnestness and seriousness onto others[CW 9i §§458, 472, 478]

TYPICAL BEHAVIOURS / PATTERNS

- Deflects seriousness with humour, often at the wrong moment
- Disrupts established arrangements — sometimes usefully, sometimes destructively
- Operates at the edges of rules and expectations
- Creates instability that others must navigate
- Reveals uncomfortable truths through indirect or provocative means[CW 9i §§460, 478]

DEVELOPMENTAL TASK

Integrate the capacity for disruption with ethical responsibility; use the gift of seeing through fixed structures to illuminate and liberate rather than merely destabilise — and develop the discernment to know when to break the pattern and when to honour it.[CW 9i §§484, 486]

Reference: Jung, C.G. — The Archetypes and the Collective Unconscious, CW 9i (On the Psychology of the Trickster Figure); von Franz, M.-L. — Shadow and Evil in Fairy Tales; Edinger, E.F. — Ego and Archetype.

NOTES

The Father

CORE ESSENCE

The archetypal principle of logos, law, differentiation, and cultural initiation; the force that calls the individual out of undifferentiated union and into the world of structure, directed purpose, and earned belonging.[CW 4 §§693, 728]

POSITIVE / MATURE POTENTIALS

- Provision of clear structure and order
- Setting of firm, fair limits
- Initiation into the wider world beyond the family
- Transmission of cultural values, laws, and earned wisdom
- Capacity to direct and focus energy toward purpose
- Encouragement of individual differentiation and self-reliance
- Modelling of disciplined, purposeful living
- Protection of the vulnerable
- Authority exercised in service of growth
- Affirmation of the child's genuine capacity and worth
- Teaching through challenge and honest expectation
- Grounding of the spiritual in practical, actionable form[CW 4 §§694, 728]

NEGATIVE / IMMATURE EXPRESSIONS

- Authoritarian control
- Conditional love — love that must be earned through performance
- Crushing of individuality in the name of order or tradition
- Chronic withholding of affirmation
- Severity without warmth
- Demanding performance beyond genuine capacity
- Law without mercy or relational context
- Emotional unavailability and distance

- Over-identification with role and achievement
- Projecting ambition onto the lives of children
- Absence — physical, emotional, or both
- Rigidity that breaks rather than shapes[CW 4 §§720, 738, 744]

TYPICAL BEHAVIOURS / PATTERNS

- Sets high expectations that leave no room for failure or vulnerability
- Withdraws approval when standards are not met
- Defines relationship through function and achievement rather than presence
- Struggles to express tenderness without undermining a sense of authority
- Continues to appear as inner judge or critic long after the external relationship has ended[CW 4 §§720, 738]

DEVELOPMENTAL TASK

Integrate warmth with authority; offer structure in the service of the other's growth rather than as an expression of control — genuinely affirming the capacity of those in one's care, ultimately having the maturity to make oneself unnecessary.[CW 4 §744]

Reference: Jung, C.G. — Symbols of Transformation, CW 5; von Franz, M.-L. — Puer Aeternus; Edinger, E.F. — Ego and Archetype.

NOTES

Note on Two Faces: The Father

The Father archetype carries two faces in Jungian psychology.[CW 4 §§693–744]

The Great Father is the initiating, authoritative, and empowering face — the paternal force that provides structure, instils genuine confidence, and prepares the individual for the demands of the world. His authority is in service of the other's development. He sets limits that open rather than close.

The Terrible Father is the crushing, withholding, or devouring face — the paternal force that diminishes rather than builds, that uses power to control rather than to initiate. Where the Great Father opens the world, the Terrible Father closes it.

Both faces are at work in the Father Complex, and both appear as inner figures long after the actual father is gone. The developmental task is to encounter the full spectrum of the paternal principle consciously — neither to idealise the Great Father nor to remain imprisoned by the Terrible Father — and to reclaim genuine inner authority no longer dependent on either the blessing or the wound of the father.

Neumann identifies the Great Father as central to the masculine principle of consciousness-formation. Distinct from the Terrible Father, this archetype activates through positive initiation: the wise elder, the king who empowers rather than consumes. The Great Father stands in structural symmetry with the Great Mother: where she generates and contains biological life, he structures and directs psychic differentiation toward individuation.

Neumann's analysis in *The Origins and History of Consciousness* provides the canonical description of the Terrible Father as the castrating, devouring masculine principle. In Jungian clinical work, the Terrible Father complex is one of the most significant sources of the inner critic and the authority wound. The Terrible Father stands in structural symmetry with the Terrible Mother: where she devours through engulfment, he destroys through petrification, criticism, and the withholding of recognition.

Reference: Jung, C.G. — Symbols of Transformation, CW 5; Edinger, E.F. — Ego and Archetype; von Franz, M.-L. — Puer Aeternus.

NOTES

The Great Father

CORE ESSENCE

The positive, generative face of the Father archetype — the wise king, the divine lawgiver, the mentor who calls latent potential into form. In Neumann's terms, the Great Father represents the masculine principle in its life-affirming function: the logos that structures and directs psychic differentiation toward its telos. He provides ordering spirit without which growth remains formless. The Great Father initiates without devouring, holding authority in the service of the other's becoming.[CW 5 §415]

POSITIVE / MATURE POTENTIALS

- Wise, discerning authority exercised in the service of another's growth
- Initiation into the deeper laws of existence and meaning
- Transmission of tradition as living inheritance, not dead weight
- Generous mentorship that cultivates autonomy in the one being guided
- Affirmation of genuine capacity and worth without condition
- Provision of clear, life-giving structure and boundary
- Drawing out latent potential rather than imposing a fixed image
- Protection that enables rather than restricts
- Integration of logos and eros — law tempered with love
- Holding of collective values in genuine service of the common good[CW 4 §728]

NEGATIVE / IMMATURE EXPRESSIONS

- Benevolent paternalism that infantilises rather than liberates

- Authority exercised in unconscious self-service disguised as generosity
- Mentorship that creates dependency rather than genuine autonomy
- Wisdom hardening into rigidity when the established order is challenged
- Affirmation withheld until worth is fully demonstrated
- Subtle inflation of the guiding role — the helper who needs to be needed

TYPICAL BEHAVIOURS / PATTERNS

- Inspires through example and earned authority rather than demand
- Provides structure that feels enabling rather than constricting
- Recognises and names the unique gifts of those under his guidance
- Transmits meaning rather than mere information or technique
- Holds boundaries without anger, shame, or need for control
- Can be depended upon without fostering unhealthy reliance

DEVELOPMENTAL TASK

Internalise the Great Father as an inner guide — an authoritative yet generous inner voice that supports differentiation without demanding perfection. Distinguish the nourishing father from the devouring father, both in the outer world and within the psyche.

Reference: Jung, C.G. — Symbols of Transformation, CW 5; Neumann, E. — The Origins and History of Consciousness; Edinger, E.F. — Ego and Archetype.

NOTES

The Terrible Father

CORE ESSENCE

The destructive, devouring face of the Father archetype — the force that inhibits growth, crushes individuality, and binds rather than initiates. The Terrible Father corresponds to Kronos who swallows his own children: the logos turned against its generative purpose, law become tyranny, structure become petrification. In Neumann's schema, this is the masculine principle collapsed into its own negative pole — the castrating, consuming father who cannot allow the new to emerge.[CW 4 §744]

POSITIVE / MATURE POTENTIALS

The Terrible Father is primarily a shadow figure; its constructive dimension lies in its function as initiatory antagonist. Encounter with the Terrible Father — whether in outer life or in the inner world — can mobilise the Hero's developmental task. Recognition of the inner Terrible Father is the necessary first step toward claiming the internal Great Father.

NEGATIVE / IMMATURE EXPRESSIONS

- Authoritarian law that punishes rather than guides
- Devouring possessiveness that prevents healthy separation
- Rigid, unfeeling demand for conformity above authentic selfhood
- Destruction of individuality in the name of tradition or order
- Humiliation deployed as a tool of control
- Emotional coldness wielded to maintain dominance
- Demands for sacrifice of the child's soul to the father's ego or ambition
- Instilling chronic self-doubt and the inner persecutory critic
- Wielding shame as punishment for autonomous expression or difference[CW 4 §§720, 738, 744]

TYPICAL BEHAVIOURS / PATTERNS

- Punishes initiative, difference, and genuine feeling as dangerous or shameful
- Uses silence, coldness, or contempt as instruments of control
- Presents obligation and duty as the only legitimate emotional currency
- Appears in inner life as the harsh, condemning inner judge or superego
- Blocks ego development through fear of paternal retaliation or abandonment
- Creates the wound that the individual must eventually face and integrate in individuation[CW 4 §§720, 738]

DEVELOPMENTAL TASK

Recognise and separate from the grip of the Terrible Father — first in the outer world, then in the inner world. The inner Terrible Father is encountered as the harsh superego, the persecutory inner critic, the voice that declares nothing is ever good enough. The task is not to destroy this figure but to differentiate from it: to hear its voice as a complex, not as truth.[CW 4 §744]

Reference: Jung, C.G. — Symbols of Transformation, CW 5; Neumann, E. — The Origins and History of Consciousness; Edinger, E.F. — Ego and Archetype.

NOTES

The Mother Archetype

CORE ESSENCE

The overarching archetypal principle of origin, nourishment, containment, and transformation; the primordial psychic pattern that carries both the life-giving and the devouring face.[CW 9i §§148, 158]

POSITIVE / MATURE POTENTIALS

- Unconditional nourishment and care
- Psychological containment and safety
- Generativity — life creating and sustaining life
- Instinctual wisdom and embodied knowing
- Connection to the cycles of nature and time
- Capacity to hold others through difficulty without abandoning them
- Grounded, receptive, sustaining presence
- Renewal after loss or ending
- Warmth and a fundamental sense of belonging[CW 9i §§158, 172]

NEGATIVE / IMMATURE EXPRESSIONS

- Devouring — consuming the identity of what it creates
- Binding through guilt, obligation, or emotional enmeshment
- Withholding nourishment as control
- Resistance to the emergence and independence of the individual
- Infantilisation — maintaining dependence rather than enabling growth
- Suffocating potential before it can become actual
- Possessiveness that masquerades as love[CW 9i §§157, 183]

TYPICAL BEHAVIOURS / PATTERNS

- Gives without limit, then experiences depletion or quiet

resentment

- Cannot allow those it loves to separate or surpass
- Creates environments of comfort that subtly prohibit growth
- Experiences the departure of others as personal abandonment
- Oscillates between overwhelming care and sudden withdrawal[CW 9i §§159, 162]

DEVELOPMENTAL TASK

Nourish without consuming, contain without binding, and sustain without suffocating; integrating the full spectrum of the Mother archetype requires the willingness to love with open hands — giving life and then allowing it to leave.[CW 9i §§188, 194]

Reference: Jung, C.G. — The Archetypes and the Collective Unconscious, CW 9i (The Mother Archetype); von Franz, M.-L. — The Feminine in Fairy Tales; Edinger, E.F. — Ego and Archetype.

NOTES

Note on Two Faces: The Mother

The Mother archetype carries two faces in Jungian psychology, both of which appear as separate entries in this Repertory.[CW 9i §§148–198]

The Great Mother is the sustaining, nourishing, containing face — the source of belonging, warmth, and life itself. She holds, feeds, and protects; she is the ground of being from which the individual emerges and to which they may safely return.

The Terrible Mother is the devouring, smothering, or withholding face — the maternal force that cannot release, that consumes rather than nourishes, that binds rather than liberates. Where the Great Mother gives life, the Terrible Mother threatens to reclaim it.

These are not opposites — they are the same archetypal force seen from two positions. Both faces are present in the Mother Complex, and both appear in the psyche as inner figures long after the actual mother. The developmental task is to encounter both without splitting — to neither cling to the Great Mother nor remain captive to the Terrible Mother — and to develop a genuine nurturing capacity that is neither absent nor consuming.

Reference: Jung, C.G. — The Archetypes and the Collective Unconscious, CW 9i (The Mother Archetype); von Franz, M.-L. — The Feminine in Fairy Tales; Edinger, E.F. — Ego and Archetype.

NOTES

The Great Mother

CORE ESSENCE

The archetypal principle of life-giving nourishment, containment, and renewal; the source of growth, abundance, and unconditional belonging.[CW 9i §158]

POSITIVE / MATURE POTENTIALS

- Unconditional nourishment and care
- Psychological containment and safety
- Fertility of body, mind, and spirit
- Generativity — life creating and sustaining life
- Instinctual wisdom
- Connection to the cycles of nature
- Nurturing of potential in others
- Emotional abundance
- Grounded embodiment
- Spiritual warmth and a sense of belonging
- Receptive, sustaining presence
- Capacity to hold others through difficulty without abandoning them[CW 9i §§158, 172]

NEGATIVE / IMMATURE EXPRESSIONS

- Smothering and over-protection
- Inability to allow separation or individuation
- Possessiveness masked as love
- Creating dependency in those it nurtures
- Defining self entirely through nurturing others
- Emotional manipulation through guilt
- Resistance to the growth and departure of those it loves
- Grief at separation experienced as betrayal[CW 9i §189]

TYPICAL BEHAVIOURS / PATTERNS

- Gives without limit until resentment quietly accumulates

- Cannot let those it loves grow beyond the nest
- Uses emotional warmth as a means of holding people close
- Creates environments of comfort that subtly inhibit growth
- Experiences the child's independence as abandonment[CW 9i §§159, 167]

DEVELOPMENTAL TASK

Allow those who are nurtured to separate and become; give freely without possession, sustain without consuming, and receive in return — honouring the full cycle of nourishment that requires both giving and release.[CW 9i §188]

Reference: Jung, C.G. — The Archetypes and the Collective Unconscious, CW 9i (The Mother Archetype); Neumann, E. — The Great Mother; Edinger, E.F. — Ego and Archetype.

NOTES

The Terrible Mother

CORE ESSENCE

The shadow face of the Great Mother; the devouring, withholding, or poisoning principle that destroys or stifles the very life it was meant to sustain.[CW 9i §157]

POSITIVE / MATURE POTENTIALS

- When integrated: fierce and legitimate protective instinct
- Capacity to set firm limits and withhold what is genuinely harmful
- Honest acknowledgement of ambivalence in love
- Recognition that destruction and creation are inseparable
- Access to raw, instinctual power
- Confrontation with the reality of mortality and loss
- Depth born through encounter with the destructive feminine
- Catalyst for the hero's individuation journey[CW 9i §189]

NEGATIVE / IMMATURE EXPRESSIONS

- Psychological devouring — consuming the child's identity
- Emotional withholding as punishment or control
- Binding through guilt, shame, or obligation
- Poisoning the well — corrupting what could nourish
- Infantilisation — keeping others permanently dependent
- Rage directed at those who seek independence
- Enmeshment disguised as love
- Suffocating potential before it can emerge[CW 9i §§157, 183, 184, 185]

TYPICAL BEHAVIOURS / PATTERNS

- Responds to the child's independence with withdrawal or rage
- Projects unwanted aspects of self onto those it nurtures

- Creates environments where growth feels dangerous or disloyal
- Oscillates between suffocating care and withholding coldness
- Activates in others the paralysis of the Wounded Child[CW 9i §§184, 185]

DEVELOPMENTAL TASK

For those in the grip of this complex: consciously separate from the devouring dynamic, grieve the nourishment that was withheld, and build a genuine inner capacity for self-sustenance — neither repeating the pattern nor remaining permanently defined by it.[CW 9i §186]

Reference: Jung, C.G. — The Archetypes and the Collective Unconscious, CW 9i (The Mother Archetype); Neumann, E. — The Great Mother; von Franz, M.-L. — Shadow and Evil in Fairy Tales; Edinger, E.F. — Ego and Archetype.

NOTES

The Kore / Maiden

CORE ESSENCE

The archetypal figure of the innocent maiden; the pre-initiatory feminine in its original state of openness, beauty, and unrealised potential. She lives in the world above — in light, in the maternal embrace, in the fullness of possibility before the descent that will transform her.[CW 9i §§306, 311]

POSITIVE / MATURE POTENTIALS

- Natural openness and receptivity to life
- Unselfconscious beauty, spontaneity, and wonder
- Deep connection to the maternal, the natural world, and the body
- Freshness of perception, undimmed by experience
- Capacity to inspire through genuine innocence and vulnerability[CW 9i §§311, 316]

NEGATIVE / IMMATURE EXPRESSIONS

- Inability to leave the maiden state — resistance to initiation, growth, or full womanhood
- Over-dependence on the mother; inability to separate and enter the world
- Naïveté mistaken for wisdom; unwillingness to encounter shadow or complexity
- Vulnerability to violation through lack of inner groundedness
- Avoidance of depth, suffering, and the demands of adult life[CW 9i §355]

TYPICAL BEHAVIOURS / PATTERNS

- Seeks to remain in a protected, childlike state of emotional innocence
- Avoids the descent — the confrontation with suffering,

shadow, or loss

- May be idealised by others (or by the self) as perpetually youthful and pure
- Relationships remain on the surface; genuine depth is deferred or feared
- The body's natural initiatory experiences are met with dread rather than received as thresholds[CW 9i §§311, 355]

DEVELOPMENTAL TASK

To accept the necessity of the descent — to allow the initiatory experience of loss, separation, or shadow to do its transforming work. The task is not to abandon innocence but to carry it consciously through the darkness, where it becomes Persephone's knowing.[CW 9i §§316, 355]

Reference: Jung, C.G. — The Archetypes and the Collective Unconscious, CW 9i (The Psychological Aspects of the Kore); Neumann, E. — The Great Mother; von Franz, M.-L. — The Feminine in Fairy Tales; von Franz, M.-L. — Individuation in Fairy Tales.

NOTES

Note on Two Faces: The Kore

The Kore and Persephone are not two separate archetypes. They are one figure, seen before and after her initiatory descent. Kore is the maiden: innocent, above-ground, not yet tested. Persephone is what she becomes when the underworld claims her.[CW 9i §§306–383]

The myth holds the structure precisely. Kore is abducted by Hades and taken underground. Demeter, her mother, searches in grief, and the earth grows barren in her absence. An agreement is reached: Persephone will spend part of each year above and part below. She is no longer simply the maiden; she has become Queen of the Underworld — mediating between the world of the living and the realm of the dead.

In Jungian psychology, this is the archetypal pattern of feminine initiation. The descent is not chosen; it is forced by life, by loss, by the inevitability of entering the world's shadow. What returns from the underworld is not the same as what descended. Persephone knows what Kore did not: that the darkness is not only destruction, but also depth, authority, and the capacity to accompany others in theirs.

The developmental task of the Kore is to allow the descent. The developmental task of Persephone is to complete the return — to carry the underworld knowledge back into the living world without remaining captive there. Both faces must be encountered honestly: the Kore cannot be bypassed in favour of forced maturity, nor can Persephone's depth become a permanent exile from the world above.

Reference: Jung, C.G. — The Archetypes and the Collective Unconscious, CW 9i (The Psychological Aspects of the Kore); Neumann, E. — The Great Mother; von Franz, M.-L. — The Feminine in Fairy Tales; von Franz, M.-L. — Individuation in Fairy Tales.

Persephone

CORE ESSENCE

The archetypal figure of the initiated queen; the post-descent feminine who has passed through the underworld and now carries the knowledge of both worlds. She rules the realm of the dead, mediates between above and below, and embodies the authority that comes only from having genuinely descended and returned.[CW 9i §§306, 311]

POSITIVE / MATURE POTENTIALS

- Capacity to inhabit both worlds — light and dark, above and below — without being destroyed by either
- Deep empathy born of genuine suffering and loss
- Authority in the face of shadow, death, and the underworld dimensions of the psyche
- Mediating function between the conscious and unconscious worlds
- Wisdom that comes only from having descended and returned
- Capacity to accompany others into their own underworld experiences without fear[CW 9i §§311, 316]

NEGATIVE / IMMATURE EXPRESSIONS

- Identification with the underworld at the expense of the living world — inability to return above
- Captivity to depression, grief, or the past; chronic heaviness or melancholy
- Seduction by darkness for its own sake — depth becomes avoidance rather than wisdom
- Difficulty sustaining engagement with ordinary life; periodic disappearance
- Using depth experience as a barrier to genuine relatedness with others[CW 9i §355]

TYPICAL BEHAVIOURS / PATTERNS

- Carries a quality of having been somewhere others have not — a certain gravity or otherness
- Drawn to liminal spaces: therapy, ritual, accompaniment of the dying, depth work
- Oscillates between periods of full engagement with life and withdrawal into the depths
- Deep attunement to others' unconscious material and unspoken suffering
- Relationships marked by genuine depth but also periodic inaccessibility[CW 9i §§311, 355]

DEVELOPMENTAL TASK

To integrate the initiatory wound without being consumed by it. The task is to move freely between both worlds — to carry the authority of the depths into ordinary life without remaining captive there. Persephone's gift is her ability to return; her shadow is the pull to stay underground.[CW 9i §§316, 355]

Reference: Jung, C.G. — The Archetypes and the Collective Unconscious, CW 9i (The Psychological Aspects of the Kore); Neumann, E. — The Great Mother; von Franz, M.-L. — The Feminine in Fairy Tales; Edinger, E.F. — Ego and Archetype.

NOTES

The Wise Old Man / Wise Old Woman

CORE ESSENCE

The archetype of earned wisdom freely offered; the inner mentor, guide, and carrier of meaning who appears at the threshold of significant developmental transition.[CW 9i §§398, 401]

POSITIVE / MATURE POTENTIALS

- Wisdom grounded in lived experience
- Capacity to guide without controlling
- Discernment — knowing what truly matters
- Holding the long view with equanimity
- Transmission of meaning across generations
- Compassionate authority
- Capacity to see and name what others cannot yet see
- Stability in the face of uncertainty
- Integration of opposites — having lived through both
- Genuine acceptance of mortality and limitation
- Presence offered as a gift, without agenda
- Service without ego investment in the outcome[CW 9i §§401, 413]

NEGATIVE / IMMATURE EXPRESSIONS

- Premature assumption of the wise elder role
- Pomposity and self-congratulation
- Using wisdom to control rather than liberate
- Withdrawal into detachment — wisdom without warmth
- Inflation — believing oneself to have arrived at final understanding
- Failure to pass on what has been learned
- Cynicism dressed as earned realism
- Using the elder role to avoid continued personal growth[CW 9i §§453–454]

TYPICAL BEHAVIOURS / PATTERNS

- Offers perspective that others are not yet able to see
- Appears at critical junctures — in dreams, encounters, literature, and synchronous moments
- Can become the identified "wise one" at the expense of their own ongoing development
- Withholds wisdom unless the question is sincerely asked
- Reflects back to others what they already know but cannot yet access[CW 9i §§401, 413]

DEVELOPMENTAL TASK

Earn the role through genuine living rather than claiming it prematurely; offer wisdom in service to the other's becoming rather than as a performance of authority; and continue to grow — recognising that the Wise Elder who has stopped learning has become the Senex.[CW 9i §455]

Reference: Jung, C.G. — The Archetypes and the Collective Unconscious, CW 9i (The Phenomenology of the Spirit in Fairy Tales); von Franz, M.-L. — The Interpretation of Fairy Tales; Edinger, E.F. — Ego and Archetype.

NOTES

A Note on Archetypes

Jung emphasised that archetypes are not fixed characters but dynamic organising principles of the psyche. There are few fundamental archetypes and unlimited symbolic forms through which they manifest.

Jung defined a complex as "a feeling-toned group of ideas" — an emotionally charged psychic structure organised around an archetypal core. Complexes are the personal emotional constellations that form around archetypal patterns through lived experience.

Archetype — Complex

Archetype = universal psychic pattern. Complex = personal emotional constellation around that archetype.

Mother archetype → Mother Complex
Father archetype → Father Complex
Anima archetype → Anima Complex
Shadow archetype → Shadow Complex

Complexes

Father Complex

CORE ESSENCE

An emotionally charged psychic constellation organised around the Father archetype and shaped by the individual's actual experience with their father or primary authority figure.[CW 4 §§693, 728; CW 8 §201]

POSITIVE / MATURE POTENTIALS

- Inner authority and genuine self-direction
- Capacity for disciplined, purposeful action
- Healthy relationship with structure and limits
- Ability to set and hold firm boundaries
- Earned confidence and decisiveness
- Mentoring capacity toward others
- Freedom from the compulsive need for external permission[CW 4 §§728, 744]

NEGATIVE / IMMATURE EXPRESSIONS

- Chronic need for approval from authority figures
- Reflexive rebellion against all authority regardless of merit
- Paralysis or submission in the presence of power
- Internalised harsh critic — the punishing inner voice
- Fear of failure or fundamental inadequacy
- Compulsive perfectionism
- Overcompensation through dominance or control
- Inability to trust one's own judgment[CW 4 §§713–728; CW 5 §§253ff]

TYPICAL BEHAVIOURS / PATTERNS

- Defers or over-reacts to authority figures disproportionately

- Recreates the father dynamic in work and professional settings
- Either submits entirely or refuses all direction
- Driven by the persistent sense of never being enough[CW 4 §§713–728; CW 8 §§201, 204]

DEVELOPMENTAL TASK

Reclaim inner authority by separating the internalised father from real authority figures; integrate the discipline without the harshness; and develop genuine self-direction that does not depend on external permission or approval.[CW 5 §§253–289]

Reference: Jung, C.G. — Symbols of Transformation, CW 5; Edinger, E.F. — Ego and Archetype.

NOTES

Mother Complex

CORE ESSENCE

An emotionally charged psychic constellation organised around the Mother archetype and shaped by the individual's actual experience with their mother or primary caregiver.[CW 9i §161; CW 8 §201]

POSITIVE / MATURE POTENTIALS

- Deep emotional intelligence and relational sensitivity
- Empathy for others in vulnerability
- Genuine capacity for nurturing
- Access to instinctual wisdom
- Connection to the felt sense of belonging
- Motivation for healing and authentic growth
- Appreciation for the life-sustaining dimension of relationship[CW 9i §§172–174]

NEGATIVE / IMMATURE EXPRESSIONS

- Idealisation or demonisation of the mother figure
- Seeking mother substitutes in other relationships
- Over-dependence on others for emotional nourishment
- Difficulty tolerating separation
- Unresolved grief, rage, or longing for the mother
- Becoming the mother one needed — smothering others
- Regression under stress
- Inability to receive care without ambivalence[CW 9i §§162–168, 184–186]

TYPICAL BEHAVIOURS / PATTERNS

- Replicates the mother relationship in other close bonds
- Experiences disproportionate emotional charge around maternal figures
- Either clings to or rejects nurturing from others

- May become excessively giving or withholding as a defence[CW 9i §§168–183]

DEVELOPMENTAL TASK

Separate the inner mother imago from real people; grieve what was not received, integrate both the nourishing and the failing aspects of the actual mother, and develop the capacity to self-mother from within.[CW 9i §187]

Reference: Jung, C.G. — The Archetypes and the Collective Unconscious, CW 9i; von Franz, M.-L. — The Feminine in Fairy Tales; Edinger, E.F. — Ego and Archetype.

NOTES

Parental Complex

CORE ESSENCE

The combined emotional constellation arising from the individual's relationship with both parents as a system — the foundational relational template for all subsequent close bonds.[CW 4 §§693, 728; CW 17 §216]

POSITIVE / MATURE POTENTIALS

- Deep understanding of relational dynamics
- Capacity for genuine repair in close relationships
- Awareness of how early patterns shape the present
- Motivation to break intergenerational patterns
- Emotional intelligence derived from navigating complexity[CW 17 §§216–235]

NEGATIVE / IMMATURE EXPRESSIONS

- Recreating parental relationship dynamics in partnerships
- Carrying unprocessed parental conflict as an internal state
- Experiencing intimate relationships through the lens of the parental template
- Difficulty holding both positive and negative aspects of each parent
- Split loyalties — unconscious alliance with one parent against the other[CW 4 §§713–728; CW 17 §§217–225]

TYPICAL BEHAVIOURS / PATTERNS

- Partners carry the emotional charge of one parent
- Conflict patterns in relationships mirror childhood family dynamics
- Feels internally caught between competing voices representing each parent
- Responds to relationship difficulty as if survival were at stake[CW 4 §§713–728]

DEVELOPMENTAL TASK

Differentiate from the parental system as a whole; develop a conscious, integrated view of both parents as complex human beings, and build relational patterns that are genuinely chosen rather than unconsciously inherited.[CW 17 §§234–235]

Reference: Jung, C.G. — Two Essays on Analytical Psychology, CW 7; Edinger, E.F. — Ego and Archetype.

NOTES

Child Complex

CORE ESSENCE

The psychic constellation organised around the individual's inner child — the emotional residue of early experience, carrying both the original wounding and the original vitality.[CW 9i §§259, 285; CW 17 §216]

POSITIVE / MATURE POTENTIALS

- Access to genuine spontaneity and play
- Emotional authenticity
- Creativity and imagination
- Capacity for wonder and openness
- Connection to core needs and vulnerabilities
- Empathy for others in their vulnerability[CW 9i §§278, 289]

NEGATIVE / IMMATURE EXPRESSIONS

- Regression to childlike dependency under stress
- Emotional reactivity disproportionate to present circumstances
- Seeking parental care in inappropriate relationships
- Feeling fundamentally small, helpless, or unworthy
- Clinging or demanding behaviour
- Self-abandonment in service of others' approval[CW 9i §285; CW 17 §216]

TYPICAL BEHAVIOURS / PATTERNS

- Regresses visibly under pressure or perceived threat
- Seeks protection or rescue rather than engaging difficulty directly
- Responds to criticism as if it were devastating
- Alternates between desperate neediness and defensive self-sufficiency[CW 9i §285; CW 17 §§216–225]

DEVELOPMENTAL TASK

Attend to and integrate the inner child — acknowledge its wounds without being governed by them, restore its vitality without regressing into it, and develop the adult capacity to parent oneself from within.[CW 9i §293]

Reference: Jung, C.G. — The Archetypes and the Collective Unconscious, CW 9i; Edinger, E.F. — Ego and Archetype.

NOTES

Family Complex

CORE ESSENCE

The overarching emotional constellation arising from membership of a particular family system — its loyalties, roles, myths, secrets, and unspoken rules.[CW 4 §§693–696; CW 17 §216]

POSITIVE / MATURE POTENTIALS

- Genuine sense of belonging and relational continuity
- Understanding of systemic relational patterns
- Appreciation of family as a formative context
- Capacity for intergenerational empathy
- Motivation to transmit what is life-giving and release what is harmful[CW 17 §§234–235]

NEGATIVE / IMMATURE EXPRESSIONS

- Unconscious loyalty to destructive family patterns
- Carrying emotional material that belongs to earlier generations
- Difficulty differentiating from the family identity
- Enmeshment — loss of individual self within the family system
- Shame or pride tied to family identity rather than personal reality[CW 4 §§713–728; CW 17 §§217–225]

TYPICAL BEHAVIOURS / PATTERNS

- Repeats family roles in other group and professional settings
- Experiences family gatherings with disproportionate emotional charge
- Feels unconsciously obligated to maintain family homeostasis
- May sacrifice personal development to preserve family loyalty[CW 4 §§713–728]

DEVELOPMENTAL TASK

Differentiate consciously from the family system; honour the lineage without being bound by it, carry forward what is life-giving, and release — with compassion — what is not.[CW 4 §744; CW 17 §234]

Reference: Jung, C.G. — Two Essays on Analytical Psychology, CW 7; Edinger, E.F. — Ego and Archetype.

NOTES

Gender-Related Complexes

Anima Complex

CORE ESSENCE

The personal emotional constellation that forms around the Anima archetype in a man — shaped by his actual relationships with women and the degree to which the inner feminine has been integrated or projected.[CW 7 §296; CW 9ii §20]

POSITIVE / MATURE POTENTIALS

- Deep emotional awareness and genuine capacity for intimacy
- Access to imagination, intuition, and symbolic life
- Authentic relatedness
- Creative receptivity
- Capacity for genuine love rather than projection
- Inner wholeness through integration of the feminine[CW 7 §§296–321; CW 9ii §§28–42]

NEGATIVE / IMMATURE EXPRESSIONS

- Compulsive idealisation or denigration of women
- Mood-driven behaviour governed by unconscious feminine contents
- Over-dependency on female relationships for emotional regulation
- Inability to sustain intimacy beyond the projection
- Seductiveness or emotional manipulation
- Passivity and loss of direction[CW 7 §§303–315; CW 9ii §§24–27]

TYPICAL BEHAVIOURS / PATTERNS

- Falls intensely in love with the projected image rather than

the real person
- Experiences mood swings driven by unconscious feminine contents
- Relationships follow a pattern of idealisation and disillusionment
- Uses women as containers for his own unprocessed emotional life[CW 7 §§303–321; CW 9ii §§24–27]

DEVELOPMENTAL TASK

Withdraw the projection of the Anima from external women; develop a conscious inner relationship with the feeling function, integrate emotional life as one's own, and relate to real women as they are rather than as screens for the inner image.[CW 7 §§321–340; CW 9ii §42]

Reference: Jung, C.G. — The Archetypes and the Collective Unconscious, CW 9i; von Franz, M.-L. — The Feminine in Fairy Tales; von Franz, M.-L. — The Interpretation of Fairy Tales; Edinger, E.F. — Ego and Archetype.

NOTES

Animus Complex

CORE ESSENCE

The personal emotional constellation that forms around the Animus archetype in a woman — shaped by her actual relationships with men and the degree to which the inner masculine has been integrated or projected.[CW 7 §328; CW 9ii §20]

POSITIVE / MATURE POTENTIALS

- Genuine inner authority and self-direction
- Clarity and decisiveness not dependent on external validation
- Capacity for independent and rigorous thought
- Assertiveness grounded in the self
- Access to purpose and directed action
- Authentic relationship with men rather than projection[CW 7 §§328–340; CW 9ii §§28–42]

NEGATIVE / IMMATURE EXPRESSIONS

- Opinionated certainty masquerading as conviction
- Harsh inner critic that undermines self-expression
- Projection of authority, intelligence, or power onto men
- Argumentative or combative relational style
- Intellectual arrogance or rigidity
- Disconnection from feeling in favour of abstraction
- Chronic self-doubt about the validity of one's own thinking[CW 7 §§331–336; CW 9ii §§29–33]

TYPICAL BEHAVIOURS / PATTERNS

- Engages in debate from fixed, unmoveable positions
- Defers to men's opinions while undermining them internally
- Experiences the inner voice as primarily critical or demanding

- Oscillates between submission to and rebellion against male authority[CW 7 §§331–336]

DEVELOPMENTAL TASK

Reclaim the Animus as an inner resource rather than projecting it; develop genuine intellectual and volitional authority from within, integrate thinking with feeling, and relate to real men as they are rather than as carriers of the inner masculine.[CW 7 §§338–340; CW 9ii §42]

Reference: Jung, C.G. — The Archetypes and the Collective Unconscious, CW 9i; von Franz, M.-L. — The Feminine in Fairy Tales; von Franz, M.-L. — The Interpretation of Fairy Tales; Edinger, E.F. — Ego and Archetype.

NOTES

Power / Identity Complexes

Inferiority Complex

CORE ESSENCE

A psychic constellation organised around a chronic sense of fundamental inadequacy — the belief, often unconscious, that one is essentially less than others.[CW 7 §§202–225; CW 8 §201]

POSITIVE / MATURE POTENTIALS

- Genuine humility
- Empathy for others who struggle
- Drive toward self-improvement grounded in reality
- Honest acknowledgement of limitation
- Sensitivity to the suffering of others
- Motivation for authentic growth rather than performance[CW 7 §§225–227]

NEGATIVE / IMMATURE EXPRESSIONS

- Chronic self-diminishment
- Compulsive comparison with others
- Inability to receive positive feedback
- Over-compensation through achievement or bravado
- Social withdrawal to avoid perceived exposure
- Deference to others at the expense of one's own needs
- Self-sabotage at the moment of success[CW 7 §§202–225; CW 18 §148]

TYPICAL BEHAVIOURS / PATTERNS

- Dismisses own contributions before others can
- Compares unfavourably and persistently with peers
- Either shrinks visibly or overcompensates with

performance

- Seeks validation constantly while disbelieving it when it arrives[CW 7 §§202–225]

DEVELOPMENTAL TASK

Separate authentic self-assessment from internalised judgment; grieve the conditions that installed the sense of inadequacy, develop genuine self-respect not contingent on achievement, and integrate both strength and limitation without distortion.[CW 7 §§227–242]

Reference: Jung, C.G. — Two Essays on Analytical Psychology, CW 7; Edinger, E.F. — Ego and Archetype.

NOTES

Superiority Complex

CORE ESSENCE

A psychic constellation often compensating for underlying inferiority — organised around an inflated sense of being fundamentally above or apart from others.[CW 7 §227; CW 9ii §43]

POSITIVE / MATURE POTENTIALS

- Genuine confidence and self-respect
- Leadership capacity grounded in real competence
- Ability to hold high standards without condescension
- Vision and ambition in service of something beyond the self[CW 7 §§227–242]

NEGATIVE / IMMATURE EXPRESSIONS

- Arrogance and condescension
- Dismissal of others' perspectives as beneath consideration
- Inability to receive feedback
- Isolation born of perceived superiority
- Entitlement in relationships and professional contexts
- Contempt masked as high standards
- Chronic disappointment that others fail to measure up[CW 7 §§227–242; CW 9ii §§43–67]

TYPICAL BEHAVIOURS / PATTERNS

- Speaks over or past others in conversation
- Treats difference of opinion as evidence of others' inadequacy
- Sets standards that function to exclude rather than inspire
- Unable to genuinely admire or be moved by others[CW 7 §§227–242]

DEVELOPMENTAL TASK

Recognise the inferiority beneath the inflation; develop genuine confidence that does not require comparison, cultivate real humility through encounter with limitation, and find belonging through equality rather than elevation.[CW 7 §§238–242]

Reference: Jung, C.G. — Two Essays on Analytical Psychology, CW 7; Edinger, E.F. — Ego and Archetype.

NOTES

Authority Complex

CORE ESSENCE

A psychic constellation organised around an intense emotional charge in relation to authority figures — expressed as submission, reflexive rebellion, or compulsive acquisition of authority.[CW 4 §§693, 728; CW 7 §238]

POSITIVE / MATURE POTENTIALS

- Appropriate respect for legitimate authority
- Capacity to exercise authority with genuine care
- Ability to relate to power without distortion
- Inner authority that does not require external permission
- Discernment about when to follow and when to lead[CW 4 §744; CW 7 §§391–398]

NEGATIVE / IMMATURE EXPRESSIONS

- Automatic submission to authority regardless of its merit
- Reflexive rebellion against all authority regardless of its legitimacy
- Compulsive acquisition of authority as compensation
- Projection of the father or mother complex onto authority figures
- Paralysis in the presence of power
- Exploitation of those in subordinate positions[CW 4 §§713–728; CW 7 §§374–391]

TYPICAL BEHAVIOURS / PATTERNS

- Behaves markedly differently with those above and below in hierarchy
- Either defers entirely or compulsively undermines authority figures
- Carries disproportionate emotional charge in workplace power dynamics

- May unconsciously become the very authority figure they feared[CW 4 §§713–728]

DEVELOPMENTAL TASK

Separate real authority from the internalised complex; develop the capacity to exercise and respond to power consciously and proportionately, to build genuine inner authority that is neither inflated nor collapsed.[CW 4 §744; CW 7 §§391–398]

Reference: Jung, C.G. — Two Essays on Analytical Psychology, CW 7; Edinger, E.F. — Ego and Archetype.

NOTES

Power Complex

CORE ESSENCE

A psychic constellation organised around the compulsive drive to control — whether oneself, others, or circumstances — typically as a defence against felt vulnerability or powerlessness.[CW 7 §§374, 381]

POSITIVE / MATURE POTENTIALS

- Genuine strength and personal agency
- Capacity to act decisively
- Healthy self-determination
- Protective strength in service of others
- Leadership grounded in genuine competence[CW 7 §§391–398]

NEGATIVE / IMMATURE EXPRESSIONS

- Controlling behaviour in relationships
- Manipulation to maintain dominance
- Intolerance of vulnerability — in self or others
- Exploitation of others' weaknesses
- Aggression when control is threatened
- Rigidity masquerading as strength
- Contempt for those perceived as weak[CW 7 §§374–390]

TYPICAL BEHAVIOURS / PATTERNS

- Micro-manages situations and people
- Becomes hostile when outcomes deviate from expectations
- Withholds information or resources as a means of maintaining position
- Responds to vulnerability in others with contempt or exploitation[CW 7 §§374–391]

DEVELOPMENTAL TASK

Distinguish genuine strength from the compulsive need for

control; encounter and integrate the vulnerability beneath the power drive, develop the willingness to be genuinely affected by others, and find security in being rather than in dominating.[CW 7 §§391–398, 405–406]

Reference: Jung, C.G. — Two Essays on Analytical Psychology, CW 7; Edinger, E.F. — Ego and Archetype.

NOTES

Messiah / Saviour Complex

CORE ESSENCE

A psychic constellation organised around the belief — conscious or unconscious — that one is uniquely destined to save, rescue, or redeem others.[CW 9ii §68; CW 7 §227]

POSITIVE / MATURE POTENTIALS

- Genuine compassion and care for others
- Motivation to contribute and serve
- Capacity for sacrifice in service of real need
- Inspiration and natural leadership
- Deep commitment to causes beyond personal gain[CW 9ii §§68–79]

NEGATIVE / IMMATURE EXPRESSIONS

- Rescuing others as a means of avoiding one's own development
- Inflation — identification with a special or chosen role
- Enabling others' helplessness rather than supporting genuine growth
- Exhaustion from carrying what belongs to others
- Resentment when those rescued do not respond as expected
- Inability to receive help or acknowledge personal need
- Grandiosity concealed beneath a guise of humility[CW 9ii §§78–126; CW 7 §§227–242]

TYPICAL BEHAVIOURS / PATTERNS

- Drawn repeatedly to people in crisis or people who cannot help themselves
- Cannot tolerate others managing without their intervention
- Defines self-worth through being needed
- Projects weakness or need onto others rather than acknowledging it within[CW 7 §§227–242]

DEVELOPMENTAL TASK

Recognise the personal wound beneath the rescuing impulse; develop the capacity to offer genuine support without taking over, allow others their own process, and attend to one's own development with the same care given to others.[CW 9ii §§115–126; CW 7 §§391–398]

Reference: Jung, C.G. — Aion, CW 9ii; Edinger, E.F. — Ego and Archetype.

NOTES

Relationship Complexes

Dependency Complex

CORE ESSENCE

A psychic constellation organised around the inability to sustain oneself emotionally, practically, or psychologically without the ongoing support of others.[CW 9i §161; CW 7 §296]

POSITIVE / MATURE POTENTIALS

- Genuine relatedness and capacity for intimacy
- Ability to receive care and support without shame
- Recognition of interdependence as a healthy dimension of life
- Warmth and emotional openness[CW 9i §§172–174]

NEGATIVE / IMMATURE EXPRESSIONS

- Clinging to relationships regardless of their health
- Fear of abandonment driving all relationship choices
- Loss of self in relationship
- Seeking a parent rather than a partner
- Inability to tolerate solitude
- Sacrificing core needs and values to maintain connection[CW 9i §§162–167; CW 7 §§303–315]

TYPICAL BEHAVIOURS / PATTERNS

- Stays in harmful relationships rather than face aloneness
- Organises life around the availability of others
- Experiences separation as catastrophic
- Presents as helpless in areas of genuine capacity[CW 9i §§162–167]

DEVELOPMENTAL TASK

Develop genuine inner resourcefulness and self-sufficiency; distinguish healthy interdependence from compulsive attachment, build the capacity to be alone without abandonment anxiety, and relate from genuine choice rather than from need.[CW 9i §187; CW 7 §§321–340]

Reference: Jung, C.G. — Two Essays on Analytical Psychology, CW 7; Edinger, E.F. — Ego and Archetype.

NOTES

Abandonment Complex

CORE ESSENCE

A psychic constellation organised around the terror of being left, rejected, or fundamentally alone — typically rooted in early relational rupture or loss.[CW 9i §§161, 285]

POSITIVE / MATURE POTENTIALS

- Deep empathy for relational vulnerability
- Capacity for genuine intimacy born of working through the core fear
- Appreciation for presence, continuity, and commitment
- Resilience developed through facing what was most feared
- Ability to hold space for others in their own abandonment wound[CW 9i §§285–289]

NEGATIVE / IMMATURE EXPRESSIONS

- Preoccupation with signs of impending rejection
- Clinging or controlling behaviour to prevent loss
- Self-abandonment to keep others close
- Testing relationships to provoke the feared outcome
- Emotional shutdown as pre-emptive self-protection
- Inability to trust continuity in relationship[CW 9i §§162–168, 285]

TYPICAL BEHAVIOURS / PATTERNS

- Hyper-vigilant to signs of withdrawal or disinterest in others
- Oscillates between intense closeness and defensive distance
- Provokes rejection unconsciously to confirm the core belief
- Cannot sustain intimacy without recurrent fear of imminent loss[CW 9i §§162–168, 285]

DEVELOPMENTAL TASK

Process the original abandonment at its source; develop the

internal security that does not depend on the constant presence of others; and build the capacity for genuine intimacy that holds both closeness and appropriate separateness without catastrophe.[CW 9i §§289, 293]

Reference: Jung, C.G. — The Archetypes and the Collective Unconscious, CW 9i; Edinger, E.F. — Ego and Archetype.

NOTES

Victim Complex

CORE ESSENCE

A psychic constellation in which the individual chronically experiences themselves as the object of others' actions, circumstances, or fate — with a diminished sense of personal agency or authorship.[CW 9ii §13; CW 7 §202]

POSITIVE / MATURE POTENTIALS

- Genuine empathy for those who suffer
- Sensitivity to injustice
- Honest acknowledgement of real harm received
- Motivation to advocate for others
- Authenticity about vulnerability[CW 9ii §§13–19]

NEGATIVE / IMMATURE EXPRESSIONS

- Chronic externalisation of responsibility
- Inability to take authorship of one's own life
- Repeated experiences of being wronged without reflection
- Using victimhood as a fixed relational position
- Resentment as a primary emotional orientation
- Helplessness as an identity rather than a circumstance
- Difficulty distinguishing genuine harm from perceived slight[CW 9ii §§13–19]

TYPICAL BEHAVIOURS / PATTERNS

- Personal stories consistently feature others as the source of difficulty
- Seeks sympathy rather than solutions
- Resists interventions that would require personal agency
- Returns persistently to evidence of having been wronged[CW 9ii §§13–19]

DEVELOPMENTAL TASK

Distinguish genuine victimisation from the habitual stance of victimhood; develop personal agency and authorship of one's own life, process legitimate grievances without making them a permanent identity, and take full responsibility for what is genuinely within one's power.[CW 9ii §42]

Reference: Jung, C.G. — Two Essays on Analytical Psychology, CW 7; von Franz, M.-L. — The Interpretation of Fairy Tales; Edinger, E.F. — Ego and Archetype.

NOTES

Martyr Complex

CORE ESSENCE

A psychic constellation organised around self-sacrifice and suffering — in which giving to excess, enduring without complaint, and placing others first becomes a central identity and a covert means of influence.[CW 9ii §13; CW 11 §520]

POSITIVE / MATURE POTENTIALS

- Genuine selflessness and care for others
- Capacity for meaningful sacrifice when genuinely required
- Endurance and resilience under difficulty
- Deep commitment to others' wellbeing[CW 11 §§520, 552]

NEGATIVE / IMMATURE EXPRESSIONS

- Self-denial as a means of generating obligation in others
- Suffering as a relational strategy
- Inability to receive or ask directly for what is needed
- Resentment concealed beneath an appearance of cheerful giving
- Guilt induction through visible self-sacrifice
- Loss of genuine needs through chronic self-neglect[CW 9ii §§13–19; CW 11 §552]

TYPICAL BEHAVIOURS / PATTERNS

- Gives visibly and then suffers the consequences — without complaint, but not without communication
- Cannot say no, and accumulates quiet resentment toward those who accept
- Uses suffering as indirect leverage in close relationships
- Resists support that would remove the grounds for martyrdom[CW 9ii §§13–19]

DEVELOPMENTAL TASK

Recognise the power and self-protection concealed within

chronic self-sacrifice; develop the capacity to ask for and receive what is needed, give from genuine abundance rather than compulsion, and find an identity independent of suffering.[CW 9ii §42; CW 11 §520]

Reference: Jung, C.G. — Two Essays on Analytical Psychology, CW 7; von Franz, M.-L. — The Interpretation of Fairy Tales; Edinger, E.F. — Ego and Archetype.

NOTES

Psychological Defence Complexes

Guilt Complex

CORE ESSENCE

A psychic constellation organised around persistent, often disproportionate guilt — the sense of having done something fundamentally wrong, whether or not actual wrongdoing has occurred.[CW 11 §520; CW 9ii §13]

POSITIVE / MATURE POTENTIALS

- Genuine moral sensitivity and active conscience
- Capacity for accountability and authentic repair
- Empathy for those affected by one's actions
- Motivation to act with greater care
- Authentic personal responsibility[CW 11 §§520, 552]

NEGATIVE / IMMATURE EXPRESSIONS

- Chronic, disproportionate guilt unrelated to actual wrongdoing
- Self-punishment as a substitute for genuine change
- Guilt as a relational mechanism — taking responsibility for others' feelings
- Compulsive apologising regardless of culpability
- Inability to forgive oneself after genuine amends
- Guilt used to avoid processing deeper anger or grief[CW 11 §§560, 659; CW 9ii §§13–19]

TYPICAL BEHAVIOURS / PATTERNS

- Apologises reflexively and excessively
- Takes responsibility for situations and feelings that are not theirs

- Cannot accept forgiveness or release guilt through genuine amends
- Uses guilt to sidestep acknowledging resentment or anger beneath it[CW 11 §659; CW 9ii §§13–19]

DEVELOPMENTAL TASK

Distinguish authentic moral responsibility from the complex; make genuine amends where warranted and release what is not truly one's own, develop the capacity for self-forgiveness, and allow guilt to serve its proper function — guiding behaviour — without becoming a permanent identity.[CW 11 §520; CW 9ii §42]

Reference: Jung, C.G. — Psychology and Religion: West and East, CW 11; Edinger, E.F. — Ego and Archetype.

NOTES

Persecution Complex

CORE ESSENCE

A psychic constellation in which the individual chronically experiences themselves as the target of others' hostility, judgment, or deliberate harm — even when evidence is absent or ambiguous.[CW 9ii §13; CW 8 §201]

POSITIVE / MATURE POTENTIALS

- Heightened sensitivity to genuine injustice
- Capacity to identify and name real dynamics of power and harm
- Protective vigilance where genuinely warranted
- Empathy for those who are genuinely targeted[CW 9ii §§13–19]

NEGATIVE / IMMATURE EXPRESSIONS

- Chronic mistrust of others' motives
- Reading neutral events as evidence of directed hostility
- Exhausting hypervigilance
- Inability to receive care without suspicion
- Escalating conflict through defensive pre-emption
- Isolation adopted as a protective strategy
- Projection of internal aggression or shame onto others[CW 9ii §19]

TYPICAL BEHAVIOURS / PATTERNS

- Consistently interprets ambiguous events as directed against them
- Builds cases from accumulated evidence of being targeted
- Responds to ordinary feedback as personal attack
- Cannot sustain trust in relationships over time[CW 9ii §§13–19]

DEVELOPMENTAL TASK

Develop the capacity to accurately distinguish real threat from projected threat; explore the internal aggression or shame being externalised, build genuine trust through direct experience, and develop a grounded rather than a vigilant sense of safety in the world.[CW 9ii §42]

Reference: Jung, C.G. — Aion, CW 9ii; von Franz, M.-L. — The Interpretation of Fairy Tales; Edinger, E.F. — Ego and Archetype.

NOTES

Narcissistic Complex

CORE ESSENCE

A psychic constellation organised around an unstable sense of self that requires constant external validation — marked by grandiosity, entitlement, and a defended core of deep shame or emptiness.[CW 7 §227; CW 9ii §43]

POSITIVE / MATURE POTENTIALS

- Genuine self-regard and healthy confidence
- Ambition in service of real contribution
- Charisma and capacity to inspire
- Vision and expansive sense of possibility
- Authentic self-expression[CW 7 §§238–242; CW 9ii §§43–67]

NEGATIVE / IMMATURE EXPRESSIONS

- Grandiosity — inflated self-importance
- Entitlement in relationships and environments
- Absence of genuine empathy
- Exploitation of others for self-enhancement
- Disproportionate rage in response to criticism or perceived slight
- Chronic need for admiration
- Inability to tolerate others' needs competing with one's own
- Shame collapse when the inflation is punctured[CW 7 §§227–242; CW 9ii §§43–67]

TYPICAL BEHAVIOURS / PATTERNS

- Dominates conversation to maintain the spotlight
- Responds to perceived criticism with disproportionate anger or sudden withdrawal
- Uses relationships primarily as mirrors for the self
- Cannot sustain empathy when it requires setting aside self-

concern[CW 7 §§227–242]

DEVELOPMENTAL TASK

Encounter and integrate the shame and vulnerability beneath the grandiose structure; develop genuine empathy through recognising the other as fully real, build self-worth independent of admiration, and move from the compulsive need to be seen to the capacity to genuinely see others.[CW 7 §§238–242, 391–398]

Reference: Jung, C.G. — Aion, CW 9ii; Edinger, E.F. — Ego and Archetype.

NOTES

Control Complex

CORE ESSENCE

A psychic constellation organised around the compulsive need to manage, predict, or direct outcomes, people, and environments — typically as a defence against intolerable uncertainty or vulnerability.[CW 7 §374; CW 8 §201]

POSITIVE / MATURE POTENTIALS

- Genuine competence and organisational capacity
- Reliability and consistent follow-through
- Attention to detail
- Ability to create order from genuine chaos
- Healthy stewardship of real responsibility[CW 7 §§391–398]

NEGATIVE / IMMATURE EXPRESSIONS

- Micro-management of others
- Inability to delegate or extend genuine trust
- Anxiety when outcomes are unpredictable
- Rigidity in the face of necessary change
- Controlling behaviour in intimate relationships
- Perfectionism as a means of avoiding vulnerability
- Exhaustion from carrying more than any one person can manage[CW 7 §§374–390]

TYPICAL BEHAVIOURS / PATTERNS

- Insists on managing all details personally
- Becomes visibly anxious or hostile when plans deviate
- Finds it difficult to rest or be present without an active task
- Relationships become subject to unilateral management rather than genuine exchange[CW 7 §§374–391]

DEVELOPMENTAL TASK

Encounter and integrate the vulnerability and uncertainty

beneath the controlling behaviour; develop genuine trust in others and in process, relinquish what cannot and need not be controlled, and find security in being rather than in managing.[CW 7 §§391–398, 405–406]

Reference: Jung, C.G. — Two Essays on Analytical Psychology, CW 7; Edinger, E.F. — Ego and Archetype.

NOTES

Citation Style Guide

Each entry carries superscript reference markers alongside its five structural elements, and a Reference line naming the works it draws on. These are signposts into your own reading — the rationale is given in "About this Book". This guide sets out the citation conventions.

References to Jung's Collected Works cite paragraph numbers (§), consistent across all editions and publishers. Jung is the primary source, and the paragraph marker takes you to the exact point in the canon — the place to begin reading him directly. The interpretive works of von Franz, Neumann, and Edinger are second to Jung. They are named at the level of the work, in the Reference line beneath each entry, with no chapter or page marker: the reader takes up the cited work and reads it in whichever edition they hold. The editions consulted in compiling this Repertory are declared in the References list at the back of this volume.

A Note on Editions

Chapter and page numbering vary between editions and translations; paragraph numbers in Jung's Collected Works do not. For that reason, entries cite Jung by paragraph and name every other work at the level of the work itself, leaving the reader to locate the material in their own copy — which is, in any case, the reading the Repertory exists to encourage. Secondary works are listed by the original date of publication, so that the development of each author's thought is visible; where a later revised edition was the one consulted in compiling this Repertory, that edition is named in the entry.

A Note on Related Entries

Several Repertory entries draw their superscript citations from the same Jung essay because Jung treats them as facets of a single archetypal field rather than independent figures. The Kore and Persephone both anchor in CW 9i §§306–383 (the Kore essay), with different paragraph picks reflecting Persephone's descent-and-return emphasis. The Mother Archetype and its Two Faces (Great Mother, Terrible Mother) all draw on CW 9i §§148–198. The Father and its Two Faces likewise anchor in CW 4 §§693–744. Wise Old Man and Wise Old Woman both rest on the Spirit-in-Fairytales essay (CW 9i §§384–455). A reader who follows the superscripts will find themselves returning to the same primary text from several entries — this is intentional, and signposts the underlying unity of the archetypal field rather than separate or redundant sources.

Author	Work	Abbrev.	Edition
Jung, C.G.	*Collected Works (CW), Vols. 1–20*	CW [vol] §[para]	Princeton University Press / Bollingen Series. Paragraph numbers (§) are consistent across all editions and publishers.
Edinger, E.F.	*Ego and Archetype*	E&A	Shambhala Publications, 1992 (orig. G.P. Putnam's Sons, 1972).
von Franz, M.-L.	*Puer Aeternus*	PA	Sigo Press, 2nd ed., 1981.
	Shadow and Evil in Fairy Tales	SEFT	Spring Publications, 1974.
	The Interpretation of Fairy Tales	IFT	Spring Publications, 1970.
	The Feminine in Fairy Tales	FFT	Spring Publications, 1972.
Neumann, E.	*The Origins and History of Consciousness*	OHC	Pantheon Books / Bollingen Series XLII, 1954.
	The Great Mother	GM	Princeton University Press / Bollingen Series XLVII, 1955.

Citation Format

Jung — Collected Works: CW [vol] §[para] e.g. CW 9ii §43 Multiple: CW 9ii §§43–45

von Franz, Neumann, Edinger — named at work level in the

Reference line beneath each entry; no chapter or page marker. Example — Reference: Jung, C.G. — Aion, CW 9ii; Edinger, E.F. — Ego and Archetype.

Where an element draws on more than one Jung volume, cite in sequence — e.g. CW 9ii §43; CW 9i §§44–46. The Reference line beneath the entry then names every work it draws on: Jung first, followed by the interpretive scholars.

Superscript Placement

Superscript markers are placed at the end of each of the five structural elements within every entry — not mid-sentence within bullet points:

Element	Superscript position
Core Essence	End of the core essence description paragraph.
Positive / Mature Potentials	End of the final bullet point in this section.
Negative / Immature Expressions	End of the final bullet point in this section.
Typical Behaviours & Patterns	End of the final bullet point in this section.
Developmental Task	End of the developmental task paragraph.

A Note on Method

The Repertory's citation apparatus carries a structural argument that is not stated in the body of the entries themselves. This note sets it out so the reader who has noticed the pattern can verify what they are seeing, and so the reader who has not yet noticed may now.

Jung does not treat archetypes as independent figures. He treats them as dynamic structures of the collective unconscious — fields — that express themselves through named figures whose identity depends on the cultural, mythic, and clinical context in which the field becomes nameable. The Kore is a field; Persephone is its named expression in the Eleusinian mystery cult. The Mother is a field; Great Mother and Terrible Mother are its polar figures in mythology and in the consulting room. The Father is a field; Great Father and Terrible Father are its facets. Jung's archetype of the spirit (CW 9i §§384–455) is likewise a field; the Wise Old Man and the Wise Old Woman are the gendered figures through whom it takes on phenomenological form.

In compiling this Repertory I have chosen to honour both the named figures and the field. Each named figure is listed as a distinct entry because the practitioner consulting the book wants the named figure they are working with — not an umbrella entry under which the named figure dissolves. At the same time, the superscript citations under each named figure draw from the same paragraphs of the same Jung essay as the figures with which they share a field. The Kore and Persephone both anchor in CW 9i §§306–383. The Mother Archetype, the Great Mother, and the Terrible Mother all anchor in CW 9i §§148–198. The Father and its Two Faces, together with the Great Father and the Terrible Father, all anchor in CW 4 §§693–744. The Wise Old

Man and the Wise Old Woman both anchor in CW 9i §§384–455.

The shared anchors are not redundancy. They are the lineage shown at the source. A reader who follows the superscripts under Persephone will find themselves reading the Kore essay; a reader who follows the superscripts under Great Mother will find themselves reading the Mother Archetype essay. The named figure is the door; the field is the room behind it. The Repertory does not state this; it lets the citation apparatus state it through what the reader does in the act of consulting.

This is the editorial method behind the structural choice. The reader who understands it will read the Repertory as a guide to the fields as much as to the figures; the reader who does not will still consult the book usefully on a figure-by-figure basis. Both are honest uses of the apparatus.

References

The reference markers throughout this Repertory point to the works listed below. Engage them directly — the Repertory signposts the reading; it does not replace it.

Primary Source — The Collected Works of C. G. Jung

Jung, C.G. (1959) The Archetypes and the Collective Unconscious. Collected Works, Vol. 9, Part I. London: Routledge & Kegan Paul.

Jung, C.G. (1959) Aion: Researches into the Phenomenology of the Self. Collected Works, Vol. 9, Part II. London: Routledge & Kegan Paul.

Jung, C.G. (1953) Psychology and Alchemy. Collected Works, Vol. 12. London: Routledge & Kegan Paul.

Jung, C.G. (1958) Psychology and Religion: West and East. Collected Works, Vol. 11. London: Routledge & Kegan Paul.

Jung, C.G. (1956) Symbols of Transformation. Collected Works, Vol. 5. London: Routledge & Kegan Paul.

Jung, C.G. (1953) Two Essays on Analytical Psychology. Collected Works, Vol. 7. London: Routledge & Kegan Paul.

Secondary Sources — Interpretive Scholarship (von Franz, Edinger, Neumann)

von Franz, M.-L. (1970) The Interpretation of Fairy Tales. Revised edition consulted: Boston: Shambhala, 1996 (C.G. Jung Foundation Book; original title An

Introduction to the Interpretation of Fairy Tales).

von Franz, M.-L. (1970) Puer Aeternus. Second edition consulted: Los Angeles: Sigo Press, 1981 (original title The Problem of the Puer Aeternus).

von Franz, M.-L. (1972) The Feminine in Fairy Tales. Revised edition consulted: Boston: Shambhala, 1993 (C.G. Jung Foundation Book; original title The Problem of the Feminine in Fairy Tales).

von Franz, M.-L. (1974) Shadow and Evil in Fairy Tales. Zurich: Spring Publications.

von Franz, M.-L. (1977) Individuation in Fairy Tales. Shambhala edition consulted: Boston, 2017 (original edition Spring Publications, Zurich).

von Franz, M.-L. (1980) Projection and Re-Collection in Jungian Psychology. La Salle: Open Court.

von Franz, M.-L. (1994) Archetypal Dimensions of the Psyche. Boston: Shambhala.

Edinger, E.F. (1972) Ego and Archetype: Individuation and the Religious Function of the Psyche. New York: G.P. Putnam's Sons for the C.G. Jung Foundation for Analytical Psychology.

Neumann, E. (1954) The Origins and History of Consciousness. New York: Pantheon Books (Bollingen Series XLII).

Neumann, E. (1955) The Great Mother: An Analysis of the Archetype. Princeton: Princeton University Press (Bollingen Series XLVII).

About Peter Twigg

I have been meditating for over forty years and have had the privilege of teaching meditation in workshops and private practice around the world. The calling began early. In my late teens, a near-miss car crash gave me a direct experience of my subtle bodies and of something — someone — looking after me. That moment has never left me. When I was twenty-four, I taught myself to meditate from a book, reading a paragraph and 'trying' to meditate and surprisingly had some intense experiences.

I met my teacher, Samuel Sagan, while studying naturopathy. Without my fully realising in my time in Samuel's school, Samuel set me on an archetypal path — that of the healer-teacher, expressed in the Greek myth by Chiron, leader of the Centaurs. When I eventually read the myth of Chiron, I read my life story. My path has been a zigzag — pulled toward career, relationship, belonging — yet I always cut back to the central thread. The inner calling has consistently proven more important than anything else.

Carl Jung's work dovetails closely with the meditation and transformation I teach. I wrote this book when I saw the impact understanding archetypes and complexes had on my students. I hope it does the same for you.

I run Peter Twigg's School of Knowing, a small school for dedicated students working at the intersection of meditation, self-knowledge, and the Western Esoteric Tradition. I have also written Truth Centred Meditation, available on Amazon in digital and print.

www.ingramcontent.com/pod-product-compliance
Lightning Source LLC
LaVergne TN
LVHW050918210926
848482LV00012B/484